Birds and Trees

by Emily C. Dawson

amicus readers

1

Amicus Readers are published by Amicus
P.O. Box 1329, Mankato, Minnesota 56002

Printed in the United States of America at Corporate Graphics,
North Mankato, Minnesota.

Library of Congress Cataloging-in-Publication Data
Dawson, Emily C.
  Birds and trees / by Emily C. Dawson.
      p. cm. – (Amicus readers. Our animal world)
  Includes index.
  Summary: "Simple descriptions describe how birds and trees are dependent
on one another. Includes comprehension activity"–Provided by publisher.
  ISBN 978-1-60753-010-7 (library binding)
  1. Birds–Ecology–Juvenile literature. 2. Trees–Ecology–Juvenile literature.
  3. Animal-plant relationships–Juvenile literature. I. Title.
  QL698.95.D39 2011
  598.17–dc22

                                        2010007289

Series Editor   Rebecca Glaser
Series Designer   Kia Adams
Photo Researcher   Heather Dreisbach

Photo Credits

Aron Ingi Ólason/Shutterstock, 18–19; Corbis/Tranz, 6, 14, 20 (b), 21 (b), 22 (ml,
bl); Dave Bevan/Alamy, cover; Getty Images, 10, 21 (t), 22 (br); Juniors Bildarchiv/
Alamy, 1; moreimages.com, 8, 21 (m), 22 (mr); Photobank, 4, 22 (tl); Shutterstock/
Florida Stock, 12–13, 20 (t), 22 (tr); Stock Image Group, 16, 20 (m)

1224
42010

10 9 8 7 6 5 4 3 2 1

Table of Contents

nest

Birds all around the world
need trees. Pied cormorants
live in Australia. They build
their nests in trees.

The red-headed weaver lives in Africa. It builds its nest in trees, too. It weaves grass and twigs into a covered nest.

hollow

The cockatoo lives in Australia. It rests in a hollow tree for shade from the hot sun.

grub

Birds need trees for food. Eastern bluebirds live in North America. They eat grubs and insects they find in trees.

The woodpecker lives in North America. It pecks trees with its bill to find insects to eat.

bill

fig

seeds

Birds help trees, too.
The pale white eye lives
in Africa. It eats fig seeds.
New fig trees grow where
the seeds drop.

caterpillar

Some bugs harm trees.
They eat the leaves.
Birds eat caterpillars
that can harm trees.

Birds and trees need each other. What would happen to trees if there were no birds? What would happen to birds if there were no trees?

Picture Glossary

bill
the horny, hard parts
of a bird's mouth

caterpillar
a larva that changes
into a butterfly or a
moth

fig
a small, sweet fruit with
tiny seeds

20

grub
the young form of some bugs that looks like a short, white worm

hollow
having empty space

nest
a place built by birds to lay their eggs

21

What Do You Remember?

Birds and trees need each other. Do you remember why? Match each bird to what it does.

Pied Cormorant

Red-headed Weaver

Pale White Eye

I peck trees with my bill to find insects to eat.

I rest in hollow trees for shade.

I weave together nests in trees.

I build nests in trees.

I eat fig seeds off of trees in Africa.

I eat grubs and insects found in trees.

Woodpecker

Cockatoo

Eastern Bluebird

Ideas for Parents and Teachers

Our Animal World, an Amicus Readers Level 1 series, gives children fascinating facts about animals with lots of reading support. Photo labels and a picture glossary reinforce new vocabulary. The activity page reinforces comprehension and critical thinking. Use the ideas below to help children get even more out of their reading experience.

Before Reading

- Talk with the child about birds and where they live. Ask: What do you know about the relationship between birds and trees?
- Discuss the cover photo and the photo on the title page. What do these photos show?
- Look at the picture glossary together. Read and discuss the words.

Read the Book

- "Walk" through the book and look at the photos. Ask questions or let the child ask questions about the photos.
- Read the book to the child, or have him or her read independently.
- Show the child how to read the photo labels and use the picture glossary to understand the full meaning.

After Reading

- Have the child retell what he or she learned.
- Use the *What Do You Remember?* activity on page 22 to help review the text.
- Prompt the child to answer the questions on page 19, *What would happen to trees if there were no birds? What would happen to birds if there were no trees?*

Index

Web Sites

BIOKids—Kids' Inquiry of Diverse Species, Bird Nests
http://www.biokids.umich.edu/guides/tracks_and_sign/
build/birdnests/

Birds for Kids—National Zoo
http://nationalzoo.si.edu/Animals/Birds/ForKids/default.cfm

Bird Nests in Trees
http://www.50birds.com/GNest8.htm

The Great Backyard Bird Count
http://www.birdsource.org/gbbc/kids